Pebble® Bilingüe/Bilingual Plus

Cómo hacer slime
How to Make Slime

A divertirse con la ciencia
Hands-On Science Fun

por/by Lori Shores

Editora consultora/Consulting Editor:
Gail Saunders-Smith, PhD

Consultor/Consultant: Ronald Browne, PhD
Departamento de Educación Elemental y de Primera Infancia/
Department of Elementary & Early Childhood Education
Universidad Estatal de Minnesota, Mankato/
Minnesota State University, Mankato

CAPSTONE PRESS
a capstone imprint

Pebble Plus is published by Capstone Press,
151 Good Counsel Drive, P.O. Box 669, Mankato, Minnesota 56002.
www.capstonepub.com

 Books published by Capstone Press are manufactured with paper
containing at least 10 percent post-consumer waste.

Library of Congress Cataloging-in-Publication Data
Shores, Lori.
  [How to make slime. Spanish & English]
  Como hacer slime / por Lori Shores = How to make slime / by Lori Shores.
     p. cm.—(Pebble plus bilingüe. A divertirse con la ciencia = Pebble plus bilingual. Hands-on science fun)
  Includes index.
  Summary: "Simple text and full-color photos instruct readers on how to make slime and explains the science behind the
activity—in both English and Spanish"—Provided by publisher.
  ISBN 978-1-4296-6106-5 (library binding)
  1. Plasticity—Juvenile literature. 2. Emulsions—Juvenile literature. 3. Cornstarch—Juvenile literature. I. Title. II. Title:
How to make slime.
  TA418.14.S5618 2011
  620.1'1233—dc22   2010042260

Editorial Credits
Erika L. Shores, editor; Strictly Spanish, translation services; Juliette Peters, designer; Danielle Ceminsky, bilingual
     book designer; Sarah Schuette; photo studio specialist; Marcy Morin, scheduler; Laura Manthe, production specialist

Photo Credits
Capstone Studio/Karon Dubke, all

Safety Note/Nota de seguridad

Please ask an adult for help when making slime./
Pídele a un adulto que te ayude a hacer *slime*.

Note to Parents and Teachers

The A divertirse con la ciencia/Hands-On Science Fun set supports national science standards
related to physical science. This book describes and illustrates making slime in both English and
Spanish. The images support early readers in understanding the text. The repetition of words
and phrases helps early readers learn new words. This book also introduces early readers to
subject-specific vocabulary words, which are defined in the Glossary section. Early readers may
need assistance to read some words and to use the Table of Contents, Glossary, Internet Sites,
and Index sections of the book.

Printed in the United States of America in North Mankato, Minnesota.
022011   006080R

Table of Contents

Getting Started 4

Making Slime. 6

How Does It Work? 16

Glossary 22

Internet Sites. 22

Index 24

Tabla de contenidos

Para empezar 4

Para hacer slime 6

¿Cómo funciona? 16

Glosario 23

Sitios de Internet 23

Índice 24

Getting Started

What's runny like glue,
but also hard like rubber?
Slime! It feels like a solid
and a liquid at the same time.

Para empezar

¿Qué es líquido como el pegamento,
pero también duro como el caucho?
¡*Slime*! Tiene la textura de un sólido
y un líquido al mismo tiempo.

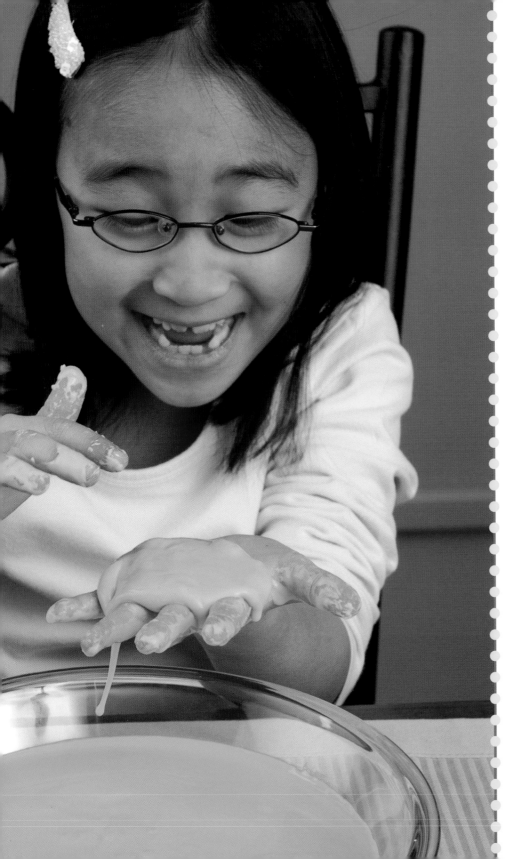

Here's what you need/Necesitarás:

dish/plato

spoon/cuchara

1 cup (240 mL)
cornstarch/1 taza (240 ml)
de fécula de maíz

food coloring/
colorante para alimentos

½ cup (120 mL) water/
½ taza (120 ml) de agua

5

Making Slime

Put ½ cup water in a large dish.

Add a few drops of green
food coloring.

Para hacer slime

Pon ½ taza de agua en
un plato grande.

Añade algunas gotas de colorante
verde para alimentos.

Add 1 cup of cornstarch
a little at a time.

Stir the mixture well
with a spoon.

Añade poco a poco 1 taza
de fécula de maíz.

Revuelve bien la mezcla con
una cuchara.

The slime should tear
when stirred quickly.

If it doesn't tear, add a little more
cornstarch one spoonful at a time.

El *slime* debe desgarrarse cuando lo
revuelves rápidamente.

Si no se desgarra, añade un poco
más de fécula de maíz,
una cucharada a la vez.

Gently rest your hand on top of the slime.

Then quickly slap the surface of the slime.

What happens?

_____

Coloca tu mano tocando apenas el *slime*.

Luego dale un golpe rápido a la superficie del *slime*.

¿Qué ocurre?

Try making a slime ball.

Push on it as you roll it
in your hands.

What happens when you let go?

Trata de hacer una bola de *slime*.

Aplástala mientras la enrollas
en tus manos.

¿Qué ocurre cuando la sueltas?

How Does It Work?

Water and cornstarch don't mix completely. The slime is mostly tightly packed bits of cornstarch. The water flows around those bits.

¿Cómo funciona?

El agua y la fécula de maíz no se mezclan por completo. El *slime* es principalmente pedacitos de fécula de maíz muy compactos. El agua fluye alrededor de esos pedacitos.

When your hand moves slowly through the slime, the cornstarch moves around. The water flows and the slime seems like a liquid.

Cuando mueves la mano lentamente por entre el *slime*, la fécula de maíz se mueve. El agua fluye y el *slime* parece un líquido.

When you slap the slime,
the cornstarch doesn't have time
to move. The water can't flow,
and the slime feels solid.

Cuando golpeas el *slime*, la fécula de
maíz no tiene tiempo de moverse.
El agua no puede fluir, y el *slime* tiene
la consistencia de un sólido.

Glossary

cornstarch—a flour-like ingredient made from corn

liquid—a wet substance that can be poured

mixture—something made up of different things mixed together

rubber—a strong, elastic substance used to make items such as tires, balls, and boots

solid—a substance that holds its shape

surface—the top part of something

Internet Sites

FactHound offers a safe, fun way to find Internet sites related to this book. All of the sites on FactHound have been researched by our staff.

Here's all you do:

Visit *www.facthound.com*

Type in this code: 9781429661065

 Check out projects, games and lots more at
www.capstonekids.com

Glosario

el caucho—una sustancia fuerte y elástica que se usa para hacer objetos como llantas, pelotas y botas

la fécula de maíz—un ingrediente hecho de maíz que es parecido a la harina

el líquido—una sustancia húmeda que puede verterse

la mezcla—algo hecho de diferentes cosas que se mezclan

el sólido—una sustancia que mantiene su forma

la superficie—la parte superior de algo

Sitios de Internet

FactHound brinda una forma segura y divertida de encontrar sitios de Internet relacionados con este libro. Todos los sitios en FactHound han sido investigados por nuestro personal.

Esto es todo lo que tienes que hacer:

Visita *www.facthound.com*

Ingresa este código: 978142961065

¡Algo súper divertido! Hay proyectos, juegos y mucho más en www.capstonekids.com

Index

ball, 14

cornstarch, 8, 10, 16,
    18, 20

food coloring, 6

glue, 4

liquid, 4, 18

mixture, 8

rubber, 4

slapping, 12, 20

solid, 4, 20

stirring, 8, 10

surface, 12

water, 6, 16, 18, 20

Índice

agua, 6, 16, 18, 20

bola, 14

caucho, 4

colorante para alimentos, 6

fécula de maíz, 8, 10, 16,
    18, 20

golpear, 12, 20

líquido, 4, 18

mezcla, 8

pegamento, 4

revolver, 8, 10

sólido, 4, 20

superficie, 12